A Life
Living MAAT

By Rkhty Amen

Title Page Picture - Symbol of MAAT

Preface

As the cradle of human civilization, Africa gave birth to profound and resilient spiritual philosophies and practices; however, the Maafa has taken its toll on Africa and her Black descendants worldwide. Many, at home and in the Diaspora, have succumbed in varying degrees and in one way or the other to the White-led global onslaught against people of Color, especially Black people. We have been pried apart from ourselves, torn from the safe moorings and life-giving instructions preserved in our civilization. Most critical of all, the cruel experiences of the Maafa have left us with little conscious knowledge of the powerful psychic/spiritual energy that lies at the core of African civilization, and how to use it to advance our security and well being. We are now, in some ways, like the ship with a damaged and impelled rudder; we simply follow the winds and currents of other people's culture. Where it's taking us, we don't know. Whether it's good for us, we don't know. We have lost the leadership role in our own destiny.

I am especially honored to have been asked to write this preface for A Life Centered Life - Living MAAT by Professor Rkhty Amen, a culturally centered African intellectual. The White privileged mindset is pervasive and resilient; it is still very much with us, and steals into every aspect of our lives. Scholarship on Africa and Black people remains overwhelmingly colonized, misinterpreted and twisted. Rkhty Amen is recovering and using ancient African paradigms to interpret reality. In *A Life Centered Life - Living MAAT* she makes a major contribution to the discussion of the most pressing issue facing Black people and humanity, religion and spirituality.

The history of religion in the West is largely a history of an institution devoted to domination and intrigue. It is literally true, holy book in one hand and a weapon in the other. How many have been slaughtered outright, and how many more have been left with deep, insurmountably distorted understandings of life, original sin, fear of death, fear of hell, fear of others, fear of living fully and freely and harmoniously.

These and the myriad of challenges to living a harmonious and sustainable lifestyle are addressed in this book. Read A Life Centered Life - Living MAAT and read it again and again. Each reading yields deeper insights and new meaning. It can change your consciousness and thus transform and empower your life, your reality.

Rkhty Amen has taken an ancient treasure and rendered it maa kheru (true of voice). Only a culturally centered and global scholar could set forth this authentic, clear text. She is one of the world's most brilliant contemporary intellectuals.

Mayibuye Monanabela, Shemese Aku Seminary

"Spirituality is above religion, above science, above social creeds (holy books). Spirituality is about the Amen, the infinite unknown, and Atum, the infinite known. Spirituality is about a love and understanding of the entire universe, an understanding that life is more than just what is here on Earth, but includes the all the multiverses and the infinite dimensions thereof. All life is animate, all life is intelligent. We exist because everything else exists. Everything is One. Therefore Spirituality is about love and respect for all life. Spirituality is about understanding oneself so that one can maintain harmony with nature and self. The Universe itself is the supreme life form. All life is animate everything is alive. All life is intelligent (intelligence is relative). There was no word in the language Medu Netcher for Spirituality, because all aspects of life were Spiritual."

Wimby, Rkhty, *The Philosophy of Kemetic Spirituality*, Chicago, Illinois, 1988

THE PHILOSOPHY OF A LIFE CENTERED LIFE
LIVING MAAT

A Life Centered Life is a way of living that is conscious thought and practice focused on the healthy growth and development of all living things.

A life centered life is not a religion, is not a science, is not a social creed, and has no holy books.

All Existence is one, one being, one nature, one essence, one spirit.

Everything is interconnected, and interdependent. Nothing exist "individual".

Everything is dependent on something else. We exist because everything else exists.

All existence is one unified whole. There is unity among all things.

All Life sustains Life. Everything that exists is sustenance for something else.

All Life is animate/alive. There is no such thing as inanimate.

All existence is light. Light is what we call energy.

All Life is energy. This is what is meant by Spirit.

What we call spirit occurs in the forms of both matter and energy.

Matter and energy are the same; they continuously change from one to the other. Energy can become condensed. While in a condensed form we call it matter and in it's uncondensed form, we call it energy.

All Life is intelligent.

All life is sacred.

A Life Centered Life focuses on understanding the interrelatedness, the links and dependencies of things with and to each other, for example, the food chain that links man and plants and animals, the elemental chain, that links particles to form elements, and the organic chain, the linking of animal, mineral and vegetable, just to name a few of the innumerable links. All existence is linked in chains of dependencies.

The survival of Life in its present form is dependent on the healthy growth and development of all things.

The Purpose of all living things is to maintain the harmonious balance, which allows everything to exist in its form and order.

The African/Kemites called this order MAAT.

NTR/NTCHER

The Kemites conceived of all the infinite manifestations of existence as being one organic whole, which they called NTR (pronounced neter or netcher). NTR is the totality of existence. In ancient Kemetic texts all existence is called NTR. All existence is ONE. The word NTR is written as a picture of a flagpole with a white banner. NTR is the origin of the word nature that has a similar meaning.

Another way of expressing the One was Atum – The Complete One, the totality of the infinite forms of existence. In the ancient language Atum means complete. Also there was the principle called Amen – Hidden, the unknown creative forces of the multiverses (infinite universes). It is no coincidence the word Amen was retained by all the Western religions, which were influenced by Kemet out of a deep respect they had gained for the wisdom of the Kemites. Then there was the concept of many NTR or NTRU (u on the end of a word indicates plurality). These are the infinite manifestations or forms of NTR, that is all the infinite forms of existence, the infinite parts of the whole, including all mass, spirit/energy, qualities, consciousness, solar systems, galaxies, Earth, sun, water, air, man and so on. In the ancient texts one finds human beings referred to as NTR, plants, animals are called NTR, the rivers and mountains, the ancient language itself is called MDU NTR "Words of NTR". NTRU was written by drawing three banners on poles, three representing plurality.

It seems that the Kemites realized that the ultimate "Cause" which brought about the "Coming into Being" of all existence was hidden and not knowable to humans. This thought is expressed by the word Amen, which means to be hidden or hide.

Every NTR is a combination of myriad NTRU which contains some essence of each in different proportions, such as atoms are said to be composed of different particles in varying degrees. For example, RA being Light/Energy is a NTR, which contains the essence of Light in the greatest proportion, yet also contains other NTRU in lesser proportions. All NTRU contain light in various proportions. Thus this is how all things are interconnected. If one were to investigate the root of all existence one would find an attribute of every NTR in every being and in everything.

Concepts and attributes are also NTR. The NTRU of the process of "Coming into Being of life" also called elements of Creation, were named and defined specifically. These would be NU - the Primal liquid in which all existence existed potentially, ATUM -The Complete One, HHU/HHUT – masculine and feminine elements of infinity, KKU/KKUT - masculine and feminine elements of Darkness, SHU - Moisture, TFNUT - air, Amen - the hidden unknown creative force of the universe.

There is a need in humans to give expression to NTR. The Kemites often referred to NTR by means of attributes or qualities of human beings and animals. Following are some of the attributes of NTR that were given names. WSIR - the attribute of rebirth, rejuvenation, growth of vegetation, was expressed or symbolized by a human wrapped as a mummy, AST - attribute of female, mother, nurturer, symbolized by a woman with a chair on her head, HERU - attribute of protector and leadership, NBT-HET - attribute of sister, wife, matrilineal descent. STESH - attribute of decaying and passing away, INPU - attribute of guardian, opener of the way, transition, symbolized by a canine or human figure wearing a canine mask, HET-HERU - attribute of beauty, love, joy, SKHMET - attribute of healing and protection was symbolized by a lioness, MAAT - attribute of harmonious balance is symbolized by an ostrich feather or a woman wearing a feather on her head, and there is RA – the light life energy of the sun which makes life possible on Earth, symbolized by a solar disk having a black dot in the middle, and AMEN – the hidden and unknown forces in the multiverses, symbolized by a ram or man wearing the mask of a ram. These NTRU are not merely attributes but "powerful energies" within us that we can use and control to bring balance into our lives.

In an ancient text called by Egyptologist, *Papyrus Leyden*, known form the late period in Kemetic history, it is written:

"Three are all Netchers Amen, Ra, Ptah; there is none like them. Concealing its name as Amen. It has Ra as a face and its body is Ptah."

Three, the indicator of plurality is actually one, because the One is plural. Amen = the infinite unknown that which is hidden; Ra = the light life energy of the universe; Ptah is the creative aspect of creation from the primal Nu. Ptah is that which creates things out of nothing into something, causing them to come into existence on Earth.

MAAT

MAAT is the laws and rules, that govern and maintain the forms of existence, and allows everything to exist in its form and order.

MAAT is the laws of combination and agreement of all the various elements that form a connected whole.

MAAT is the laws of equilibrium among all the differentiated forms of existence.

MAAT is the harmonious balance, the agreement and adaptation of all the various parts/elements of creation to form a connected whole.

Order is the life cycle in which a thing maintains itself in its form (its existence). Form is the "composition" of a particular energy or mass.

Elements are the building blocks of life in whatever form they occur. Humans know some of the elements and some are unknown.

Agreement and harmonious balance between the elements or forms produces a healthy growing and developing whole. For example, all the elements or parts of the human body work together to produce a healthy body.

The elements of the creation process work together to produce the multiverses and the orderly movement of all the celestial bodies.

Health is the harmonious balance of the parts of the whole.

Illness occurs when the parts are out of balance.

MAAT was present at the Sep Tpy "First Coming into Being". It is written in the ancient Kemetic text: "MAAT endures, it is unchallenged since the beginning".

Humans do not know all the laws that govern life; therefore, there is a need to study the science of life, which our ancestors called MAAT. The study of MAAT explores how NTR becomes different forms and maintains these forms. The Maatian path of study examines the process of differentiation of the whole, and how the connection is maintained. These things need to be studied so people can work to insure that all existence can exist in harmonious balance with each other.

SYMBOL OF MAAT

MAAT is symbolized by a woman wearing a wing feather of a male ostrich on her head and sometimes by the feather alone. There are then two main aspects of this symbol, a female and a male aspect. In a famous relief from Kemet, which depicts the Day of Judgment at the end of a person's earthly life, MAAT is shown placed on a scale and weighed against one's *ib* (person's consciousness). The MAAT feather in this representation symbolizes balance and harmony depicted by female and male combined. The scene also implies that one's consciousness should be light as a feather. The color white of the feather symbolizes light and pureness. The fact that MAAT is both male and female is highly significant. The female is the one who nourishes the young, the caregiver, the mediator/harmonizer in the family, the first teacher of MAAT to the young. The female is a natural embodiment of MAAT in the sense of caring for, nourishing, mediating, and harmonizing in the family, the community and the nation. The male ostrich wing feather combined with the female represents balance and harmony.

MAAT ON MANY LEVELS

MAAT is realized on every level of existence. MAAT can be said to be the link between planes or levels of existence. MAAT is realized in the cosmic plane, and in the human conscious and subconscious plane. It is realized in nature, and MAAT is realized on the human social plane, and the all the myriad planes of existence. All planes/levels are interconnected. They cannot be separated.

The ancient Kemetic texts say that MAAT was present at the beginning of the process of "Coming into Being". As the process continues for eternity MAAT is those laws which allow the multiverses and all therein to exist in their forms and orders. Humans do not understand this process even though humans also are creators and participate in the process.

All things in Nature work in accordance with the laws of MAAT to sustain themselves and continue to grow and experience health/balance. All things in Nature are governed by natural orders and cycles of things, which maintain a harmonious balance and in turn allows for everything to continue to exist in a healthy, growing and developing state.

HUMAN/SOCIAL PLANE

The purpose of humans is to maintain MAAT on Earth.

MAAT is doing that which is accordance with maintaining the harmonious balance in nature. That is, taking care of the Earth and all things thereon.

MAAT is doing that which promotes health, growth and development in all people and all of nature.

To do MAAT is to respect the sacredness of life.

To do MAAT is to treat the whole Earth as a sacred place. It benefits us to take care of the Earth because it is the source of sustenance for Earthly beings.

To do MAAT is to work to bring about harmony in everything that is in your environment.

To do MAAT is caring about all living things.

To do MAAT means to exist in harmony with nature, to work to produce a healthy natural environment.

To do MAAT is to do that which is Right and Just and Good.

To do MAAT is to share and give to others.

To speak MAAT is to speak openly and truthfully. Everything we do and say matters. Everything we do or say either helps or hurts something or someone else.

To do MAAT is to have compassion towards others and toward nature.

To do MAAT is to do and say what is right in respect to that which promotes harmony and balance. This applies to what you do in your family, in your community, in your nation and in the world.

To do MAAT is to strive to achieve good character in oneself and be a model for others.

To do MAAT is to do Good and always strive to bring good into the world.

To do MAAT is to work to make life better for others and by doing so you make life better for yourself.

To do MAAT is to correct imbalance and fight against Isft (the Kemetic word for wrong doing).

According to the ancient teachings, to do wrong, speak falsely is an abomination even to oneself and goes against the grain of any stability or success in life. Reward and success never comes from doing wrong. What do people and all living things receive from doing MAAT? They receive ankh, uja, seneb, nefer. The English language cannot literally translate these words, however, a close meaning may be, Life, Prosperity, Health, and Happiness. Doing MAAT creates an ideal environment for life, prosperity, health and happiness to exist for each person individually, and for all people. These are the things, which the Kemites desired for all people to achieve. Ankh, Uja, Seneb, were the most often written words in the ancient language Medu Neter. These words were also the most common greeting used by people. Because they believed in the power of the spoken word, we know that the Kemites believed that speaking, writing and thinking these words would bring these conditions into being.

MAATIAN GOVERNANCE

MAAT was the basis of social order and also the main principle of governance. MAAT is the highest form of political consciousness. Imagine if you will a society, which emulated and only rewarded the truly righteous man/woman, only those who do good and bring good into the world. Such a society would automatically discourage people from doing wrong because there would be no profit or benefit in that activity. MAAT was the principles by which the Kemetic nation and its communities attempted to govern themselves. The leader of the nation was called the Nasut Bity, he or she was ideally a "morally right leader" who lead according to the principles of MAAT otherwise he/she would not be allowed to govern, nor be accepted by the people. The office of Nasut Bity required one to be MAAT. The morally right leader was the representative of MAAT on Earth. Imagine a world where leaders were required to lead according to the tenants of MAAT, Right, Truth, Justice, Good, Balance, Compassion, promoters of healthy, growth and development for all their people and the Earth. That was the ideal of governance by MAAT in Kemet. There were written texts of instructions on how to govern by MAAT. Many of these have survived and can be studied by us today.

In order for Kemet to function as a Maatian society, all the people needed to have knowledge of the Maatian order. The idea of knowledge being hidden to the people would not have worked in Kemet. That is why knowledge/information was inscribed in large, bold writings on the walls of buildings, temples, houses, streets, everywhere, for all the people to read. In actuality, in order for any society to function well all the people need knowledge of its most fundamental rules and principles. When the people are not educated the society cannot function in a Maatian way and will fail on most levels. A society functions only as well as it people are educated to its principles. Kemet was not a perfect place, as no place is, mainly because of the "human element", however, Kemet as a nation always strove to attain MAAT.

The "human element" was and is the most crucial factor in any government. People are capable of great good, and great evil. In the ancient Kemetic *Book of Two Ways*, it says that the causes of wrongdoing are ignorance and immaturity. Most importantly however, is the fact that the Kemites were aware of one's ability to live a Maatian life, and that the goal they as a society worked towards.

People, they realized, were not limited to one circumstance, as in Western thought, to things like environment, culture, race, genetic inheritance, social status, but Kemites believed that humans continually recreate themselves. Thus, it was thought that people could overcome unfavorable conditions and fulfill one's purpose or mission in life despite obstacles. In another book called *Book of Coming Forth by Day* (also known as *The Book of the Dead*), there is a passage entitled "to purge oneself of wrongs which one has committed". Reciting this passage allowed a person making their transition an opportunity to correct wrongs done or mistakes made in life.

The ancient writings from Kemet contain words of wisdom, which can help people today to strive for MAAT. Self-reassessment makes it possible for man to continually create himself anew. The Kemites wanted to be "on the boat of the NTRU in one's lifetime. They desired to become "Maa Kheru", which means: "true of voice" while on Earth. Living a Maatian life on Earth was prerequisite for being pronounced "Maa Kheru" and "justified" on the final judgment day, before one's transition. Interestingly, in the many depictions of the *Day of Judgment*, there has not yet been found a scene with an unbalanced scale. This is an indication that there was a belief that a person had the opportunity to change, that ones fate is not limited, because of ones circumstance on Earth, nor limited in other realms after life on Earth. There is always an opportunity to overcome one faults and circumstance and to do MAAT.

On Earth people go through different stages of growth: In Africa there is a custom of renaming oneself. This is done by receiving a new name after significant changes in one's life. A person could be given a new name at an initiation, such as the time when a young person entered into manhood or womanhood, or when one reached or attained eldership. When a person did something very special or did something extra ordinary in their life, they are given a new name in a sacred ceremony and recognized as such by the community. A person does not always have to remain the same person they had once been; one becomes a "new person" through growth and development. This ability to grow and change is very important. Renaming oneself is also a custom common to many indigenous cultures. It is important to note here that in collective societies, such as we have in indigenous cultures, there is the same concern for the individual as in so-called highly individualized societies in the Western world. In collective societies the individual receives much attention and concern and is an important focus in the community. Whereas in the West, the individual is isolated and alone and little attention or concern is given to people, because everyone is too busy being an individual.

MAAT is that which people aspired to in life. In the tomb biographies of ordinary people words similar to these below are commonly inscribed. The following passage is one example of a biographical inscription that is found on nearly all tombs in Kemet. This one is from the biography of a man named Idi:

"I went forth in my city; I went down in the nome. I did MAAT for the possessor of MAAT.

I satisfied NTR because I loved NTR.

I was loved by my father and praised by my mother. One, his sisters and brothers loved.

I repeatedly spoke MAAT.

I spoke MAAT. I did MAAT.

I gave bread to the hungry, clothes to the naked.

I never did any evil to anyone; I never thwarted anyone's inheritance.

I was a revered one before NTR and before the people."

These lines express what people thought was most important in life. This is what people wrote on their tombs. Imagine if you can a society where the person of MAAT was the highest model of humanity. MAAT was not a written Law, nor a divinely inspired prophecy; it was instilled in people through practice in a collective society. Presently, Kemet is the longest lasting nation of which we have written record, having lasted more than 10,000 years of written history.

LIFE CENTERED NOT GOD CENTERED

It is perhaps because of the Kemitic idea of life as being One organic whole, as expressed in the concepts of NTR, that Western Egyptologists came to the conclusion that NTR is the same as their concept of god. However there is a fundamental difference between the concept of god and what is meant by

NTR. In order to understand this difference it is important to know that the Kemites did not have a god concept. Their way of life is not monotheism, the reverence of one god, nor was it pantheism, namely, the idea that "god is everywhere", or "god is in everything". It is not henotheism. It is not polytheism, the belief in many gods. When the Europeans first saw the NTRU portrayed as animal-headed beings, drawn on walls and papyrus, and saw what appeared to be people in the act of giving reverence to them, they thought that the Kemites were worshipping animals and animal headed beings. They also thought that they were polytheist that is, believers in more than one god. Later, Egyptologists began to think of the NTRU more as different forms of a god, which indicate merely certain qualities of a god. In the reliefs depicted on the walls, the Kemites were not worshiping anything. Worship is a practice that implies giving honor and respect to a god or gods, the NTRU however are not gods. NTRU are innate attributes/elements of all things that exist.

Indeed, none of the above Western terms can be applied to the Kemetic way of life. In all the above concepts, what western religions mean by god and what is meant by NTR is fundamentally different. Western religions make a very definite distinction between creator, man and nature. In Kemet there was no difference between these. They were the same, same essence, same nature, same energy/spirit. The basis of Kemetic spirituality we can say was "a life-centered life" versus "a god-centered life". In Kemet all existence becomes the object of one's love, concern and commitment. All existence is NTR. This world-view is founded in the concept of MAAT, which requires a reverence and commitment to the well being of all living things, the same kind of commitment that Western religions give to their god. Here indeed lies the very essence of Maatian spiritual practice. There is a very essential difference between what is meant by god and what is meant by NTR. For if a man worships a god who is himself an entity, a being, that god becomes the object of one's love, concern and commitment. One's focus is not on Nature/All Existence but is instead focused on a god concept. That is to say, the Christian god is the object of Christian life and worship. Allah is the object of Islamic life and worship. In some Eastern religions, individual enlightenment-Nirvana is the object of one's life. The center of Western religion is god and next to god, man becomes the supreme life form, and the only intelligent one, and it is for man that god exists, for his salvation. Kemetic spiritual practice was centered not on any particular entity or god but rather on the healthy, growth and development of all life.

Western religions proclaim one god to be a creator of all existence. In Kemetic spiritual practice creation was in fact conceived of as a process and not as a single event, which happened once at the beginning of time, but instead, a process that is forever happening. The word for the creative process in the Medu Neter was KHPR (pronounced khe-per). KHPR is symbolized by a dung beetle that was imagined as pushing the sun RA across the sky thus representing the life cycle of the sun and of humans. As in this symbolism, the beetle pushes its dung and buries it in the Earth, which becomes a fertilizer for plants, starting the process of birth and growth of plant life. Coming into being/manifesting is a process, and is infinitely happening within and by means of all NTRU, including humans.

RELIGION

Western people are religious. Religion is about a god. It is the devotion to and worship of a god or "supernatural" forces, which some people believe govern their lives. God is also conceived as a being separate from and higher than the rest of living things. Religion most often originates from human created institutions. It is through these institutions that a "belief system" spreads and which ultimately controls a doctrine about a god. All religions have a set of written doctrines or holy books. Kemites on the other hand were NOT religious but lived a life based on the principles of MAAT, which had no doctrines or holy books.

Not all cultures of the world have a god concept nor are all world cultures religious. Some world cultures do have the idea of a single Creative force. However, the idea of one god, is a relatively new thought for indigenous people. Most of the cultures of Earth did not have this concept. How different cultures relate to life is diverse. Cultures have different thoughts on the coming into being of life. There are so many different ways of looking at this idea. In fact, the Kemites themselves had many different stories of how existence came into being, and they believed that all their many "creation stories" were good, interesting and possible. Fundamentally they thought this knowledge was "amen" hidden and unknown to humans.

Some African and other indigenous cultures, due to westernization and a loss of knowledge of their own traditional way of life, have given up their spiritual practices and replaced them with Western religions. Some people are ashamed of their traditional way of life because they no longer understand them or even know of them. They do not understand the power or energy of their traditions and do not know that there is "science" and true power embodied in them. It is good and wise to know the ways of one's ancestors. The way of life of the ancestors sustained their societies for thousands of years and are important to the continued existence of their descendants.

RITUAL

The people of the cultures of Africa appear to have lived in a "Spiritual" world, that is a world which many dimensions/planes of reality are connected, and where all life forms participate therein simultaneously, a world which incorporates not only the known but also the unknown, that which has passed away and that which is yet to be. Everything people do is linked with all of NTR. In the thought of indigenous people there was no separation, everything was conceived as interconnected and interdependent. Their rituals were about maintaining the connections between the different life forms and different dimensions. In the language Medu Neter, there was no general word for space and there was no general word for time. Yet there are words for different kinds of time and different kinds of space. The Kemites functioned in many different dimensions of time and space of which linear time and cyclic time and space are only two kinds. Consider time in dreams, imagination, and intuition, and dejavu. Space and time are multidimensional. Ritual connects the doer of the ritual with other space/time dimensions. Ritual can bring consciousness into or expand out of a physical state. People can experience other levels of consciousness by practicing ritual. Rituals expand our consciousness to other aspects of life and other realities. Through rituals such as libation, the "Htp di Nsut" evocation at the ancestral shrine, community communion, we can expand our level of consciousness, transcend time and space and eventually unite with the multiverses.

Our ancestors have taught us through example that ritual is important. Rituals are performed at birth, initiation, rites of passage at every stage of life, and for transition into the next stage of existence. Rituals are preformed when people need to make changes or to solicit help from the ancestors. Ritual connects people with cosmic consciousness. Ritual is about moving energy. For example, a ritual dance actually moves the space around the dancers and enables them to transcend their Earthly space into another dimension or space. Ritual is about manipulation of or moving matter/energy. Ritual can even change energy/matter from one form to another, allowing humans to take on other forms.

Several Kemetic rituals concerned reciprocity, that is, sharing with nature that which we continuously receive from it. Kemites and other indigenous people understood the notion that "we exist because everything else exists". They understood the reciprocal process which sustains all life. Perhaps the most sacred of all the words in their language were the little offering rituals of reciprocity, called the "*Hotep di Nsut*". The *Hotep di Nsut* means an offering that the maintainer of MAAT gives. People visited the shrines of the NTRU and the tombs of their ancestors regularly. There they poured libations and presented offerings to nature. The eldest son or eldest daughter of a family usually carried on the care of the tomb or shrine, and preformed the ritual libations. However, care for the ancestors was not only a family concern but also a community concern, a duty in which everyone in the community participated. This ritual practice is common throughout Africa today, surely part of our ancestral heritage. The ancestors share a common bond with people on Earth. According to Kemetic writings, ancestors exist in different levels of consciousness and in different dimensions of time/space and can move in and out of these planes. Thus, they are just as much a part of our lives as those on Earth, and are remembered daily. We hear them, see them, and speak to them everyday. The rituals at the ancestral shrine were practiced throughout Africa, during the great migrations, and are a central part of African daily life to this day.

Here is an interesting ritual that was described to the author by a Ghanaian artist named Kwame Nkrumah. He related that when a drummer sets out to make a drum, he first considers the innate spirit of the tree (source of his wood). The tree is alive and therefore sacred. Before he fells the tree and chops up the tree for wood, he pours libation and begs forgiveness for this act. This act is done not only for the tree but also for the sake of the drum so that the spirit/energy of the tree will enter the drum. Thus the man links his work of making the drum with the Spirit world. When the drum is made, the drum for him is alive. The drum will "speak" to the people. When the drum is finished a ritual called Ayane is played to awaken the drum; it is music to please the spirits. The drum will be used by people to do good.

LIFE CENTERED LIFE EDUCATION

In Kemet MAAT was the first education that a person received from their parents while still in the womb and once born into this world. MAAT was first taught by the mother and then in the extended family. Instructions on Maatian ethics, moral teachings, were focused on how to live a life-centered-life. These instructions were begun in infancy, not as a set of religious doctrines or government laws but as practices modeled by the family and community, demonstrating how to live one's life on Earth. The knowledge of MAAT was instilled in each child as a prerequisite teaching for everything else they would learn in life. This way is very different from a religious or parochial education used in religious cultures, which focuses on a god concept and religious doctrines. These instructions were taught and modeled in the home and community by the mothers and the fathers and the larger extended family. Maatian ethics were learned behavior, modeled in the family.

There is a large body of literature from Kemet, which gives instructions concerning MAAT. The Moral Instructions were taught in school through reading and writing of Kemetic literature. Kemet was a literate society. Male and female students learned to read and write. Students copied the wise teachings to learn the art of writing, and at the same time learn the profound messages from the passages therein. There were also other creative ways of teaching, which are common to most Africa cultures. Some of those are, drama, dance, music, and rituals. People easily learned, and understood lessons taught using these methods. The NTRU were portrayed in drama and dance to teach people concerning them. In these dramas a priest would wear a mask of the head of an animal in order to represent the attribute symbolized by the animal. Servants of NTR (Priests) also portrayed NTRU in certain rituals, wherein the attributes of the NTRU were invoked. This practice has remained popular in African rituals over thousands of years. This method of teaching is very effective and engaging. Very complex concepts are effectively taught in this way.

The moral teachings of MAAT would instill in people a sense of responsibility to community and society, to Earth and all existence. Maatian education offered a set of guidelines for development of self, society and all life. It was important that all the people in the society were educated in MAAT so that the society could function in a state of well being for everyone and everything. If all people in the society had not had this knowledge, then the society would not be able to function well.

It is the purpose of education, which ultimately makes it Maatian. The most fundamental difference between Western and African education is its purpose. The purpose of Western education is to train people to function within a Capitalist system, to fill the ranks of the workforce as capitalists, to consume the material things produced by the society, to acquire position, money, power, to gain control over others and the planet. Quite differently, the purpose of Maatian education is the protection and development of all life, society, self, and to respect and care for others and the Earth, to show compassion and create harmonious balance and health.

The means to an end influences the end result and also the desired end will influence the means to it. Therefore it is important to study the educational processes, the departments and disciplines that are aimed at producing Maatian people. The processes of Maatian education would include disciplines that stress MAAT and self awareness, which is central to understanding self and others and nature and people's relationship to each, in order that one can fulfill one's mission in life. In Maatian education that purpose would be learning to live in harmony with NTR/Nature. Unlike Maatian education, Western educational institutions include disciplines, departments and courses that stress individualism and mastery over nature, the purpose would be service to self (self-aggrandizement).

Another Maatian aspect of education is whole self-learning. It is logical, rational, intuitive, spiritual, physical and metaphysical. It is an education, which operates on the assumption that there are many realities beyond the empirical. Yet Western science does not operate in this mode of inquiry. Western education up till now has been purely deductive, purely analytical. The ideas that were expressed by the scientist Albert Einstein, may never be fully comprehended by Western thought processes (he had gone beyond Western thought processes). There is, however, a heightened interest today in the sciences of parapsychology, psychoenergetics, (Psychoenergetics is the study of the interaction of consciousness, matter and energy) and quantum theory. Every year millions of dollars are spent on research in these fields. However, one reason that these sciences are of interest in Western societies is because of their possible military applications. Europe and the West recognize and understand the superior power of these sciences. These sciences also known as the occult, or magic, are the peculiar knowledge base of indigenous people. These sciences attempt to incorporate the myriad aspects of existence, in order to bring them into synthesis. There is great vision and great power in them.

Maatian education is focused on understanding the interrelationship of all things. It is through understanding MAAT that a third aspect of education reveals itself, namely, synthesis. Synthesis means: bringing together, combining of parts into, or so as to form a whole. Therefore students need to study the relationship between everything, the laws governing the connection between things and how the connecting can be maintained for the health and balance of all.

Concerning what can be called Maatian ethics, Dr. Maulana Karenga, a well known scholar of Maatian ethics, has written: "Understanding MAAT really must be the basis of an African education. Moral ethical and spiritual study should be prerequisites for all other studies, and especially for the sciences." If Maatian ethics were practiced then people would ask questions and consider the consequences before creating weapons of mass destruction, which could destroy life on the planet   Earth, as we know it.

WESTERN EDUCATION

Now let us ask what is not a Life Centered Life education. First consider that prayer in school is not life centered education. Prayer is an aspect of parochial education. The desire for prayer in school is in fact part of a "god centered" movement occurring in Western cultures. In Western religious cultures, there is a debate going on about whether or not to have prayer in school. Some people argue that having prayer in school is equivalent to putting god in education. The problem here is, whose god? Because people practice different religions and have different beliefs, and some people do not have a god concept at all. Is it not right to force people to participate in a belief system that is not their own? Prayer in school would in essence be a daily reflection on the Christian god, and against the spiritual practice of many people.

In Western education learning is both logical (here referring to the logic of Aristotle) and analytical. Analytical, or by analysis, pertains to resolving or separating into elements or constituent parts. The analytical process proceeds by deductive reasoning based on our immediate experience and what is perceived to our senses.

"The object of all science", wrote Albert Einstein, "whether natural science or psychology is to coordinate our experiences and to bring them into a logical system. The only justification for our concepts is that they serve to represent the complex of our experiences; beyond this point they have no legitimacy. I am convinced that the philosophers have had a harmful effect upon the progress of scientific thinking in removing certain fundamental concepts from the domain of empiricism, where they are under control."

According to The Oxford Dictionary, the word science comes from the Latin word "scire" meaning to know; to separate, to distinguish. It is any branch of, or department of systematized knowledge considered as a distinct field of investigation or object of study. Thus, Western science is composed of hundreds of separate disciplines. For example, biology, chemistry and philosophy are separate disciplines. Physics, mathematics and astronomy are separate. Medicine, psychiatry, psychology are separate disciplines. In the West, disciplines are taught separately as if these could really be separated as if there was little continuity between them. It is believed that a doctor can treat only a specific physical illness of a person without treating the whole person, other related problems would be referred to another specialist.

Indigenous medical practices are wholistic, they treat the whole person including their spirit/energy not only their physical body. It is just recently that the West is witnessing an attempt at convergence of the different sciences. It is beginning to understand that in order to be a good biologist you have to know not only biology but physics and chemistry, quantum theory and so much more as well.

Now deductive, analytical science has its benefits, for in order to understand the whole, one does need to understand the parts; but one cannot actually know a part without placing it in a whole, because the essence of everything is in each part and nothing exist individual. Presently, after centuries of scientific thought there is a focus on understanding synthesis. The problems of Western science, however, go beyond that of the purely deductive, empirical scientific method, but consist in its inability to grasp the non empirically given component in scientific knowledge.

Western education is confined to two-dimensional linear concepts of space and time, what Hunter Adams, a leading scholar in Neuro/Mind Science, calls the Western singular reality. According to Adams:

"Now everything Western/European people do, their every action, culture, social institutions, organizations, even nations, is either consciously or unconsciously influenced by certain basic assumptions, which are based on their "singular reality." "(1) The first assumption is that there is no reality beyond the senses; (2) All existence is non-living. Life is limited to single-celled organisms, to man; (3) Man is only a physical being. He has no nonphysical aspect; (4) Man is the supreme life form and the only intelligent one; and (5) Death is final: absolute termination of human consciousness."

Hunter H. Adams Unpublished Paper

This view can be appropriately called a "Human-Centered" view of life with man in the center and everything in life is all about man. A Maatian education is not "man centered" but will be "Life Centered".

Now is the time for the people of the earth to look at the possibilities of a Maatian education that, as we have seen is very different conceptually from a European education. Western education is intended for the minds and spirits of the children of Europe, not the children of non-European cultures. And here we are now, our children are being raised in Western educational institutions, being taught a way of living so different from that of our ancestors, in institutions which function on different principles and work in different ways. Thus, we are cast into a European mold of thought and practice. Our way, a Life Centered Life way, the Way of MAAT is no longer followed. Let us take back control of educating our children and teach the principles of MAAT; we will then practice our Way and make our special contributions to the world.

A rocket ship going to, and landing on the Moon or even to Mars is a great feat, but we must also know that there are greater things that people can do. Going to the moon in a machine propelled there by fuel and fire is not the only way to get there. However, we can never go beyond the machine, we cannot think if we continue in the European/Western system of education and understanding of science and life. We must free ourselves from this and "Come into Being" into our own reality.

Once we return to MAAT we can create a new world, a new science, a new life, a new planet, an Earth which thrives and sustains all its life, one whereon every person can grow and develop and reach their highest potential. Only Maatian education, one embodying moral and spiritual principles can do this. The process of despiritualism which the world is faced with today is very destructive. It may be that the planet will only survive if we return to our spiritual path, the way of living MAAT. It is written in the ancient Kemetic book of a man named Kheti:

"Follow in the footsteps of your ancestors, for the mind is trained through knowledge. Behold their words endure in books. Open them and read them and follow their wise counsel. For one who is taught becomes skilled. Do not be evil for kindness is good (Maat). Make the memory of you last through the love of you." *The Husia*, by Dr. Maulana Keranga

COMPONENTS OF HUMANS

How did the Kemites perceive of human beings? What was their place in the natural order? People were perceived as spiritual beings the non-physical/energy aspect enlivening the physical/matter aspect. African people have a saying that "we are spirit having a human experience". In Medu Neter the physical/matter aspect of a man was called JET. The non-physical aspect that enlivens the body was known as KA. The KA was depicted in the language by a picture of upraised arms embracing the vital life force or energy. Ka can be compared with what the Orientals call Chi, the people of the Kalahari call Num, the Indians (of Asia) call Prana. The KA is the aspect of man that remains near by on Earth after one has made their transition to the next stage of life. It is said that the KA stays near Earth, and inhabits pictures or statues of the person. It was to the KA that libations were poured. It also dwells in another dimension of consciousness.

A second aspect of man was the BA. The BA was depicted by a Jaribu bird. It is the non-matter, in other words spirit/energy that gives each individual his unique selfness. The BA is depicted as flying between dimensions/planes after a person's transition from this Earthly life. In the tomb of a Kemetic scribe named Pa-Heri, it is said, that in the next stage of a person's existence, a person's BA can take the form of anything that one desires.

A forth aspect of a person is one's AKH symbolized by a crested Ibis. The AKH is an eternal energy/spirit. In the ancient texts, it is said to mingle with the indestructible stars. The AKH can be evoked to act on behalf of the living. The ancient Kemites even wrote letters to their AKH/ancestors, requesting their assistance for problems here on Earth. The letters that the Kemites wrote to their ancestors were addressed to the AKH. In the ancient language, AKH or AKHU were words used to name ancestors.

There seems to have been no fear of the ancestors in Kemetic thought (no such idea has been attested to in any writings thus far). Even the tombs robbers had little fear of robbing the tombs. However, certain illnesses were believed to be brought on by those ancestors who were not content. Also some illnesses were thought to have been brought about by certain NTRU (there was the idea of spiritual non physical causes). Indeed, it may be that the ancestors had more to fear from living, for example; the fear that when one's name ceases to be called or remembered, then one ceases to exist in this Earthly realm and then an important bond is broken. This is why Nasut Bity Seti 1 said:

"To do that which is of value is eternity. A king who is called forth by his works does not die. He who plans for the future is not forgotten for his name continues to be remembered because of it. To live for eternity is to be remembered for eternity."

Nourishment of the above aspects of man was important, as with everything in nature. This nourishing was done ritually. There were the libations and the food offerings. Nourishment comes in other forms beside food and water. On the walls of the tombs at Beni Hassan in Kemet, are shown hundreds of individual 'postures' or martial stances being done and presented as nourishment to NTR. Everything one does on Earth could be done as, or thought of as nourishment. The offering scenes depict all activities of man's daily life being presented as offerings to NTR, through physical exercise, dance, martial stances, playing music, not only was the body nourished but also the KA. It is through rituals that the KA is brought in union with the physical body. Nourishment is necessary for life. Food nourishment sustains life, activity sustains life, beautiful things are a form of nourishment which sustains life. Most importantly, the KA, and the AKH were nourished by propitiation at the ancestral shrine. Food was brought there and libations were poured there, and names were evoked there. Kemites thought that speaking a name causes it to live.

TRANSITION

What the West calls death was considered simply another stage of life. In actuality, death has no place either spatially or temporally. Human consciousness exists in other forms after the body's dissolution. The Kemites referred to these forms as KA, BA, AKH and JET. There was a large body of literature, which dealt with the continuation of life, although this literature had multiple purposes. This we know because the literature additionally relates to Earthly as well as celestial existence as well as multi-dimensional existences. These texts were not solely funerary texts as many Western scholars have described them. For example, the so-called *Book of the Dead* was called in Medu Netcher *The Book of Coming Forth by Day/Light*. This book was intended to be used by those living on Earth as well as by those who had transcended the Earthly dimension. Many passages from the texts specifically relate to "those who are living on Earth." Some passages state, "these words are useful for one on Earth." Once again, reiterating the importance of knowing how to live a Maatian life on Earth. *The Book of Coming Forth by Day* was available to almost anyone. It could also be used merely for a person's own enlightenment. For the book to be used for the transition into the next Life, there were passages which prescribed rituals to bring about the unification of RA and WSIR, in other words, the union of energy spirit and matter. The transcended person becomes WSIR and joins RA in its passage through the Cosmos doing the infinite cycle of life being reborn each day for eternity. In the *Book of Amduat*, the corpse of the NTR RA is equated with the corpse of WSIR. Regeneration takes place in many dimensions. The SAH (mummy) symbolized the space between Earth and the next life. Through one's SAH a person remains connected to the Earthly dimension. SAH may be thought of as being in a state of suspended animation, ready at any moment to resume its life, to be reborn. Mummification was preferred by people of Kemet, but not actually necessary to secure a blessed after life. Most people were buried directly in the Earth without a coffin.

MEN AND WOMEN IN THE SERVICE OF NTR

Concerning the men and women who served in the temples in Kemet, they were not "priest" as in the religious sense. There are special words or titles in

Medu Neter for people who performed different functions in the temples, all of which are translated by the Egyptologists as "priests". Here are some of those titles, along with an attempted translation into English of the terms (note: vowels were not written in Medu Neter.).

Hm NTR– Servant of NTR

Hm Ka – Servant of the Ka

Hry hb – One who is over the rituals

Stm - One who recites the rituals

Irt –kht= Doer of Things

Were Kemetic "priest" similar to Christian priest? How much of an individual was a hm? Several facts have come to light from looking at the tomb biographies from Kemet.

Hm (pronounced hem) were normally married and had families.

Both men and women were Hm. The female term was Hmt.

To be Hm one had to have maturity and wisdom, and much training into the way of MAAT.

The Elders of a family, father, mother, eldest son, or eldest daughter or the elder leaders of the community were naturally assigned to be Hm representing the family or the community.

Hmu (*u* for the plural) held positions and responsibilities outside the temple responsibilities. They were family and   community people.

Inside the temple, doing ritual was the main duty of the Hmw. Temples were also places where the community participated in rituals, festivals, celebrations, like, the New Year, Ancestor's day, astronomical observations, Harvest festivals, and community fellowship. The rituals were written down on the temple walls (although originally they were probably passed down orally). There is no evidence of there being such a thing as a monk or ascetic as one finds in Eastern and Western religions, since the Hm was not devoting himself to a god or to his own individual enlightenment, instead to the whole of his/her family, community and nature, which requires active involvement in collective life. No one thus far from the ancient texts is known to have lived their lives solely in the temple.

FALL OF KEMET

Nothing on Earth is permanent in its physical form. Civilizations pass through the same cycles as every other living thing. They come into being, grow, begin the decaying process and then pass away, only to be reborn in one form or another. How shall we interpret the fall of this great civilization, guided by the concept of MAAT, defeated by a seemingly less spiritual force? Perhaps at first glance Kemet may appear as the weaker, and the nations founded on the concepts of religion and individualism and aggression, appear to be the stronger. This is not so. Let us not forget that thus far Kemet is the longest lasting civilization presently known to humans; no one actually knows the how old, however it is safe to say Kemet lasted more than 10,000 years without a break, as attested in it's written texts. (The life span or duration of the some ancient civilizations contemporary with Kemet was only a few centuries or of few thousand years.) No people fought longer and harder against Isft than the people of Kemet.

 Kemet was brought to its end by many thousands of years of brutal wars, and relentless attempts at occupation by foreigners. The people of Kemet waged a mighty protracted struggle of resistance against their enemies but in the end they were completely worn out and their resources depleted. Toward the end, the people also began abandoning the way of MAAT, and perhaps began practicing the way of life of foreigners. Also the Nasut Bity (Kemetic moral leader) became more focused on war with the foreigners out of necessity than on Maatian leadership. After the fall of Kemet in 600 A.D. there occurred the beginning of the great migrations to other parts of Africa and the world. Today throughout the continent of Africa there remain many aspects and reminiscences of Kemet's profound and great cultural heritage, a heritage that began, not only in the Hapy Iteru (Nile River Valley),

but dates back much further into Africa's past. The Kemetic way of life emerged from southern and central Africa and at the end Kemet merged back into Africa. There remains to this day a strong cultural unity dating from Africa's beginnings to the establishment of Kemet, to the African societies of today.

TIMELESS CYCLES FOR AFRICAN PEOPLE

In this world today, we have begun to forget the way of MAAT. However, we will always be able to refer back to the abundant writings from Kemet to study the teachings of our African ancestors, for guidance and understanding. Their writings were intended for us, for prosperity. "Let us open their books and read them" says an ancient text. It is not that we have forgotten but that we no longer acknowledge our traditions, our way. The way of MAAT is innate in our being. MAAT is the primal/biological urge of indigenous people.

The people of Kemet called themselves remetch "the people". In tomb reliefs many different nationalities of people are represented. In the Tomb of Rameses, there are six nationalities of men depicted. Southern Africans nations are shown having the same color, manner, and dress at the Kemites, though they are designated as different national-groups. Whenever foreigners came into the country, they were "Kemitized", adopting the culture and ways of Kemet. On the contrary, the people of Kemet did not adopt foreign customs or foreign gods, while on the other hand foreigners did adopt Kemetic customs, dress, practices, etc. Furthermore, maintaining Kemetic control of Kemet was always at the forefront of

Kemetic foreign policy. The Kemites advocated independence of their country.

Advocating independence for one's country must not merely imply separation and concern for only one group of people, because the survival of all people depends upon all people uniting into one family, the "People of Earth" family. All people have a Maatian or moral responsibility to be concerned about the fate of all people not just their single nation. Unity and unity of purpose does not imply that everything must be alike. It does not mean forcing integration of people, ideas and cultures. That we are all related, namely being the same species, does not make us exactly the same. There is diversity of species in nature. There is diversity of languages and cultures. Everyone is not the same. Humans can be compared to a tree with roots and a trunk with many branches, twigs and leaves. The tree must remain whole to be healthy we cannot allow the destruction of the branches of the human family for then in actuality the tree would die. Harmonious balance of the branches is needed for good health of planet earth. And therein lies the essence of MAAT, the adaptation of all the various parts/elements of creation to form a healthy connected whole. Agreement between the different parts as to produce unity of effect or an aesthetically pleasing whole. The parts of the body produce the body's harmony and the parts of the universe produce universal harmony, by each group of people on Earth understanding their relationship to the whole.

To live a life centered life, MAAT, means understanding the differences of the people of the planet Earth and making sense of our differences by seeking understanding of each other. We need to recognize and appreciate that a variety of meanings and interpretations, our differences are what ultimately makes life MAAT. A particular way of living, a worldview, differs for the people on Earth, no matter how ideally our own unique identities serve us, one's own orientation and worldview is not the same for all people. Life does not require that all people be the same. Relationships do not imply conformity, the parts of the whole need to continue to exist in their many forms, in order for the whole to exist. Along with this must come an understanding of self and a real appreciation for what we are. This is essential to our existence and the continued existence of the planet Earth. Only people who know and understand themselves can be real contributors to maintaining MAAT on Earth.

We must find our way back to MAAT, to save ourselves, and life as we know it. We envision the Way of MAAT to be the path to the best life for people on the planet Earth. But what does that mean in practical terms? What does this mean for us living today and tomorrow? It may be difficult for those who have been educated from a Western perspective to understand MAAT. To some it may seem and ideal from a "primitive" past, and especially thought of as being unscientific. It is difficult for people who are emerged in Western culture or involved in religions or political nationalism to a cause, to become interested in a Maatian way of life. In other words, people want immediate fixes and immediate solutions to their problems and seldom want to take the time to change self, family, society and the world. It is easier to destroy or break something than to build or fix. People talk of war, making wars with people of different cultures, or beliefs, making war against nature. War is destructive and never solves any problems. What if instead of making war all people of Earth were committed to making peace with dedication and seriousness? There needs to be schools of thought, think tanks, university courses to study peace making. Throughout millennium much scholarship has been devoted to the study of war. It is now time to change our focus and study making peace.

Some say that now people must focus on modernity, the future, on science, technology. We now seek to find ways to incorporate new technologies into a modern worldview. Some may ask: how is pouring libation on the Earth going to liberate indigenous people? How is having an ancestral shrine going to bring back the deceased? How is saying a blessing over a meal going to change the fact that it's going to be eaten? How is looking at the sun and saying "thank you" going to insure its continual risings? We need to think about what is the purpose of scientific study.

What could be more scientific than to know how to work to maintain life eternally, to nourish and balance life, to take care of that which sustains us, to help all mankind to thrive on this Earth, to build rather than destroy, to stop and reflect upon our ancestors and remember them and give reverence to them because of what they did for us, to stop and reflect upon those things which sustain our lives and stop taking everything for granted, to function as one cosmic whole, rather than in one of linear time and space, to be able to experience other realms of reality beyond our five senses? The answer is the to live the way of MAAT.

REPEATING THE BEGINNING

NOTES:

1. Kemet is the ancient name for the country that is presently called Egypt. Kemet means the Black Land in reference to the Black people who lived there. The name of the people was Kemeytu meaning Black people. This Nile Valley civilization lasted for more than 10,000 years as attested in their written history, however, no one really the how it is. Kemet crossed paths with all the ancient civilizations of Africa, Asia, Europe and the Americas and influenced them in many ways with their advanced knowledge and culture.

Kemet is important for study because it has the largest body of written literature of any ancient civilization. Its writings cover all topics. Today we can read the ancient Medu Neter (Egyptian Hieroglyphs) and learn from the wisdom and knowledge of these ancient Africans.

2. Medu Netcher or Medu Neter means words of NTR, or words of nature.

3. Mankind, humans, human beings - Excuse the use of these words, please note that in English when speaking about people the reference is exclusively to male not female, thus the use of *man*, even the western god concept is male. In non-Western cultural thought and language male and female are complementary and reference to people is not exclusive of one or the other.

4. Indigenous people - a group of people native or "original" to a place where they live, earliest inhabitants of a place who have lived there for thousands of years. The people of Kemet were native to the continent of Africa, according to their writings they migrated from southern Africa.

38727546R00031

Made in the USA
Middletown, DE
24 December 2016